Becoming a Mosquito

by Grace Hansen

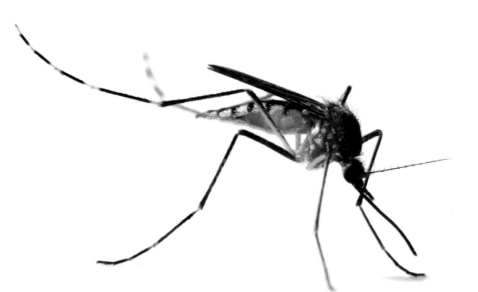

Abdo
CHANGING ANIMALS
Kids

Abdo Kids Jumbo is an Imprint of Abdo Kids
abdopublishing.com

abdopublishing.com

Published by Abdo Kids, a division of ABDO, P.O. Box 398166, Minneapolis, Minnesota 55439.
Copyright © 2019 by Abdo Consulting Group, Inc. International copyrights reserved in all countries.
No part of this book may be reproduced in any form without written permission from the publisher.
Abdo Kids Jumbo™ is a trademark and logo of Abdo Kids.

052018

092018

THIS BOOK CONTAINS
RECYCLED MATERIALS

Photo Credits: iStock, Science Source, Shutterstock

Production Contributors: Teddy Borth, Jennie Forsberg, Grace Hansen

Design Contributors: Dorothy Toth, Laura Mitchell

Library of Congress Control Number: 2017960560

Publisher's Cataloging-in-Publication Data

Names: Hansen, Grace, author.

Title: Becoming a mosquito / by Grace Hansen.

Description: Minneapolis, Minnesota : Abdo Kids, 2019. | Series: Changing animals |
    Includes glossary, index and online resources (page 24).

Identifiers: ISBN 9781532108174 (lib.bdg.) | ISBN 9781532109157 (ebook) |
    ISBN 9781532109645 (Read-to-me ebook)

Subjects: LCSH: Mosquitoes--Juvenile literature. | Animal life cycles--Juvenile literature. |
    Insects--Metamorphosis--Juvenile literature. | Animal behavior--Juvenile literature.

Classification: DDC 571.876--dc23

Table of Contents

Stage 1

All mosquitoes begin as eggs.

Mosquitoes lay their eggs in

calm water.

4

5

Some eggs float freely.

Other eggs clump together.

They sit on top of the water.

7

Stage 2

The eggs hatch within 48 hours. A newly hatched mosquito is a **larva**.

9

The **larva** eats very small matter in the water. It grows and **molts**.

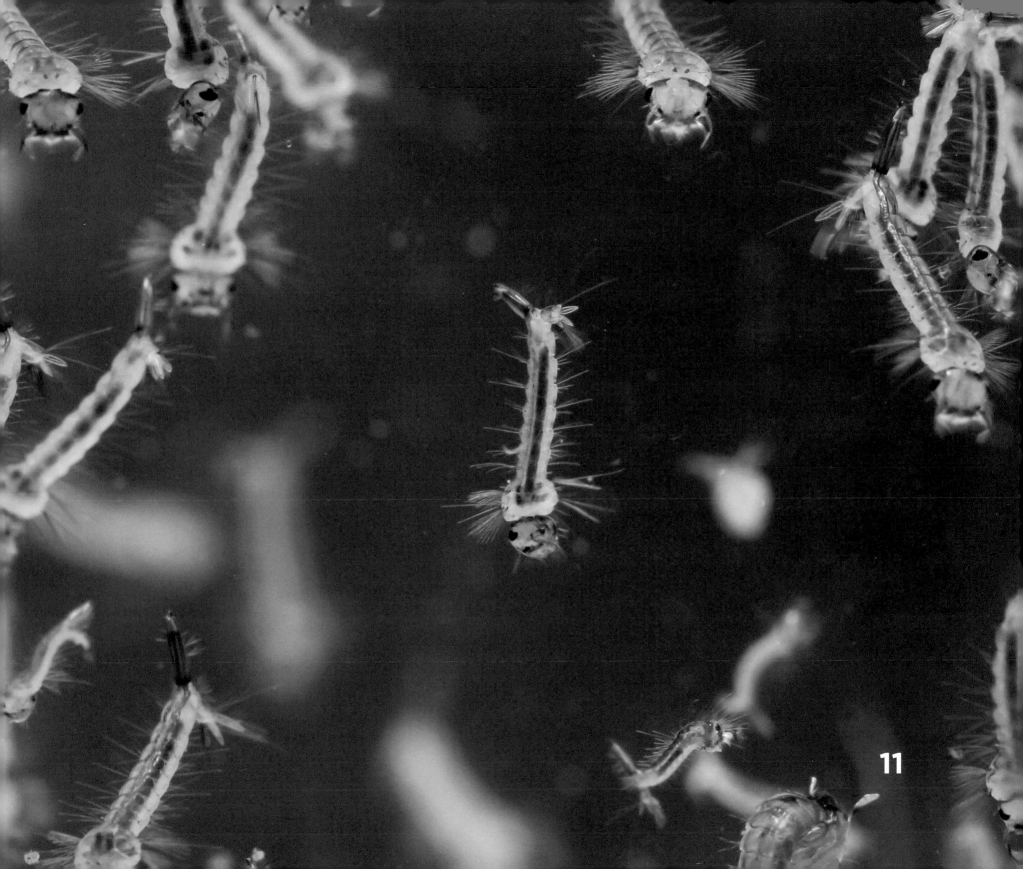

11

Stage 3

The **larva molts** four times.

It changes into a **pupa**

during its fourth molt.

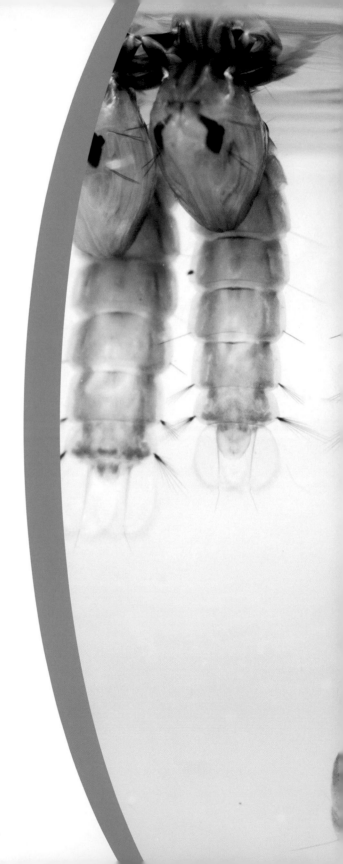

The **pupa** takes this time to rest. It does not eat. But lots of changes happen!

Stage 4

This stage lasts only about 2 days for some **species**. When the mosquito is ready, it splits its **pupal** skin. It is an adult now!

The mosquito floats on the surface and rests. It lets its body dry out and harden.

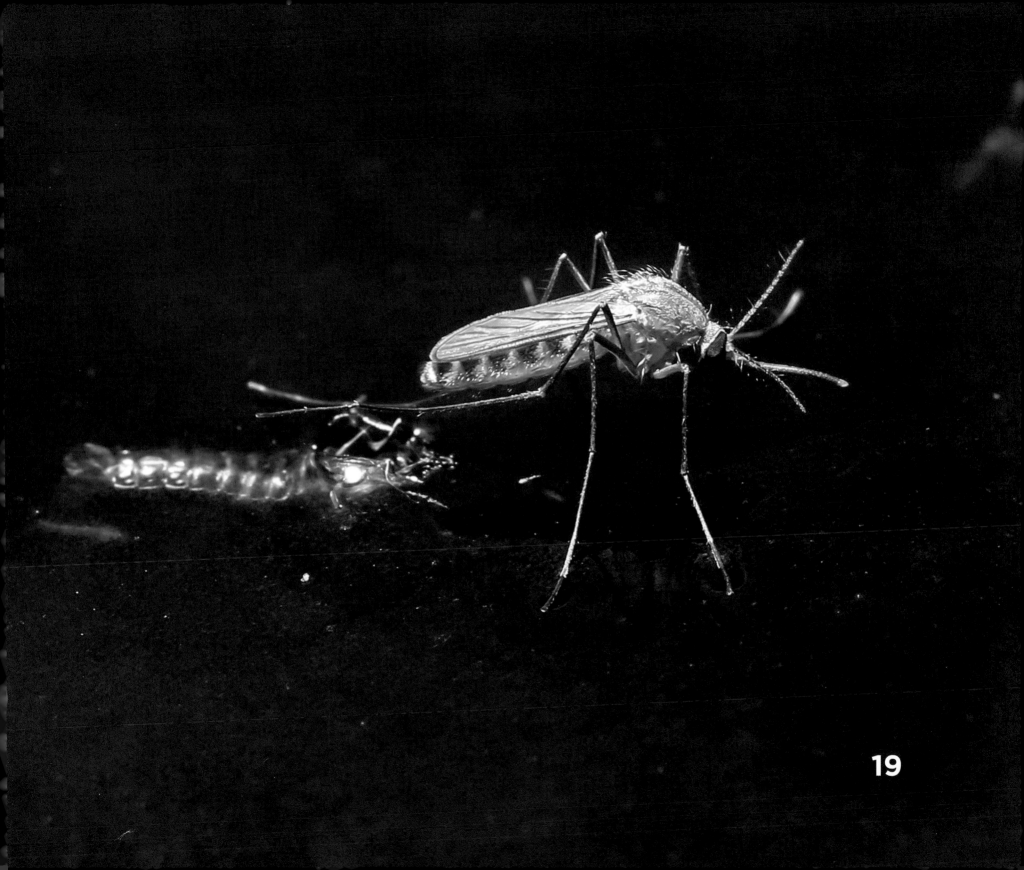

19

After 2 or 3 days, mosquitoes are ready to eat. They feed on the blood of other living things. Soon, females will lay more eggs. And the cycle will start again!

More Facts

- Only female mosquitoes suck blood! Males feed on plant sugars. Females need blood to lay eggs.

- Mosquitoes can live anywhere from 2 weeks to 6 months.

- Many animals love to eat mosquitoes, like bats, birds, and frogs.

Glossary

larva – the early form of an animal that at birth or hatching does not look like its parents and must grow and change to become an adult.

molt – to shed skin that will be replaced by new skin.

pupa – an insect that is in the stage of development between larva and adult.

species – a group of living things that look alike and can have babies together.

Index

Abdo Kids
ONLINE
FREE! ONLINE MULTIMEDIA RESOURCES

Visit **abdokids.com** and use this code to access crafts, games, videos, and more!

Abdo Kids Code:
CBK8174

24